Road Riding in the Columbia River Gorge

A guide to the best road rides in The Gorge

By Clint Bogard

Cover photograph:

Riding the St. Petersburg Loop in The Dalles on a spectacular sunny day.

Copyright 2007 by Clint Bogard.
All rights reserved

www.gorgecycling.com

ISBN 978-1-4357-0516-6

Table of Contents

Ride	Distance	Elevation Gained	Page
Hood River to Mosier	14 Miles	1148 Ft	10
Eastside Road	11 Miles	646 Ft	15
Glenwood Loop	43 Miles	2643 Ft	19
Vista Ridge Loop	37 Miles	4140 Ft	24
Rowena Crest	27 Miles	2203 Ft	31
The Dalles Lollipop	43 Miles	3640 Ft	36
Lost Lake Loop	33 Miles	3431 Ft	41
Trout Lake 52 Mile Loop	52 Miles	4166 Ft.	47
St. Petersburg School Loop	28 Miles	1403 Ft.	52
Klickitat River	40 Miles	1464 Ft.	57
Laurence Lake	25 Miles	2276 Ft.	62
Whatum Lake	31 Miles	3579 Ft.	68
Odell Loop	19 Miles	1378 Ft.	73
Goldendale Loop	68 Miles	2000 Ft.	78
Appleton Loop	29 Miles	2400 Ft.	83
Parkdale Loop	35 Miles	2200 Ft.	89

Appendixes:

Hood River Lodging, Page 94

Hood River Bike Shops, Page 96

Hood River Restaurants, Page 96

Introduction

The road riding in the Gorge must be ridden to be believed. The Gorge features majestic scenery, remote mountain roads, excellent road surface and very few cars. On many routes you will only see a handful of cars; I did a 30 mile loop recently where I only saw 2 cars!

The scenery includes fruit orchards, the Columbia River, Mt. Hood, Mt. Adams and the rivers and corresponding valley's of all the tributaries feeding the Columbia. In terms of wildlife it is not uncommon to see deer, coyotes, bald eagles, elk, wild turkey and even the rare bear or mountain lion.

Whether you're an experienced cyclist looking for a new riding area to explore or a beginner seeking scenic rides, the Gorge has a selection of rides for you.

Many cyclists choose to make Hood River a base camp for their trip to the Gorge. Hood River is one of the coolest towns in the northwest with great bike shops, restaurants, and night life. If you want to make your trip a 'multi-sport' adventure, Hood River also features world class windsurfing, kite-boarding, mountain biking, kayaking, trail-running, white-water rafting, mountain climbing (Mt. Hood & Mt. Adams) and hiking.

Hood River is the host to the Mt. Hood Cycling Classic, the largest stage race in the Pacific Northwest. In 2007 this will be a women's qualifying event for the Olympics. The criterium stage of the race is an excellent spectator event.

Mt. Hood Cycling Classic: Criterium Stage in Downtown Hood River

Mt. Hood Cycling Classic: Criterium Stage in Downtown Hood River

For those in good riding shape, looking for loops with lots of climbing, check out:

> Lost Lake
> Vista Ridge
> Glenwood Loop
> Goldendale Loop
> The Dalles Lollipop
> Trout Lake Loop

If you seek long flat/rolling rides, check out:

> Klickitat River
> Rowena Crest

For beginner riders, check out:

> Hood River to Mosier
> Eastside Road from Panorama Point
> Rowena Crest (slightly longer ride)

For those riders looking for even bigger rides, I've included a 'variations' section for some rides that suggest ways to add additional miles to the ride or loops that you can easily combine to form longer rides. Some of the juiciest combinations include:

> **Appleton Loop + Goldendale Loop**
> 85 Miles with over 5,000 ft of elevation gain
> **Glenwood Loop + Trout Lake Loop**
> 95 Miles with over 6,000 ft of elevation gain
> **Lost Lake Loop + Vista Ridge Loop**
> 58 Miles with over 7,400 ft of elevation gain
> **Parkdale Loop with an 'out-and-back' to Laurence Lake & Cooper Spur Ski Resort**
> 63 Miles with over 5,000 ft of elevation gain
> **Whatum Lake + Lost Lake + Vista Ridge**
> 68 Miles with approximately 9,000 ft of elevation gain

The Gorge is also famous for world-class windsurfing and kiteboarding. One of the reasons windsurfers love the Gorge is the number of summer days with 20+ mph winds. While this is great for wind powered sports it can make for unpleasant road riding; especially on certain routes. The following rides are the most sheltered on windy days:

- Lost Lake
- Laurence Lake
- Vista Ridge
- Glenwood Loop
- Trout Lake Loop

The west wind is typically the lightest in the early morning and strongest from 2 PM to 6 PM.

A note about the elevation profiles for each ride: I have normalized these elevation profiles so every elevation profile represents 53 miles on the X axis and 3100 feet of elevation gain on the Y axis. Because all the elevation profiles have been normalized you should be able to easily compare the elevation profile of each ride.

Start location for each ride

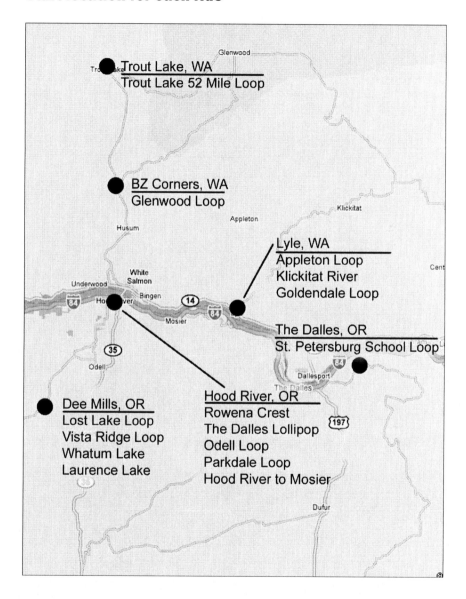

Hood River to Mosier

Description

This ride features spectacular views of the Columbia River as you roll along the historic Columbia Highway. You will go through the Mosier Twin Tunnels twice. Most of this ride is closed to cars. The road surface is probably the smoothest you'll ever ride. This ride is an 'out and back'.

The historic Columbia Highway

Turn-out over-looking the Columbia River

Ride Stats
Distance: 13.91 Miles
Elevation Information:
    Total Elevation Gained: 1148 Ft
    Starting Elevation: 145 Ft
    Maximum Elevation: 523 Ft
Ride Format: Out and Back
Estimated ride time: 45 Minutes to 75 Minutes
Season: March through November.
Good to ride on a windy day?: No.
Start Location: Discover Bicycles/Mt. View Bikes, Hood River.
Drive time to start of ride from Hood River: 0 Minutes
Quality of road surface: 10
Overall ride quality: 8
Difficulty: 3

Elevation Profile

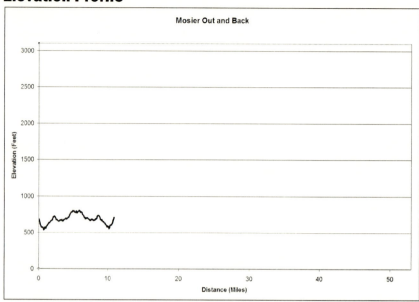

Aerial View

Map

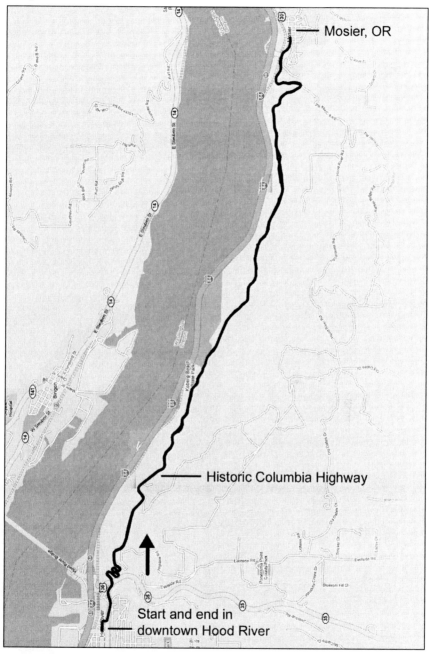

Turn by turn instructions

- **0.0 Miles:** Start at Discover Bikes/Mt. View Bikes 116 Oak Street, Hood River, OR 97031
- **0.0 Miles:** Go west on Oak Street
- **0.1 Miles:** Turn left on State Street
- **0.5 Miles:** Cross Rt. 35
- **0.5 Miles:** Continue East on Old Columbia Highway
- **1.2 Miles:** Stay left on Old Columbia Highway
- **6.0 Miles:** Turn left on Rock Creek Road
- **6.7 Miles:** Turn left onto 1st Ave.
- **6.9 Miles:** Enter Downtown Mosier
- **6.9 Miles:** Turn around and go back the way you came

Eastside Road from Panorama Point

Description

On this ride, you'll roll through the heart of orchard country--pears, apples, and cherries. You'll also be treated to spectacular views of Mt Hood on the way out and then spectacular views of Mt. Adams on the way back. You probably will not see more than a handful of cars. This ride is an 'out and back'.

Riders on Eastside Road

Ride Stats

Distance: 10.90 Miles
Elevation Information
  Total Elevation Gained: 646 Ft.
  Starting Elevation: 682 Ft
  Maximum Elevation: 800 Ft.
Ride Format: Out and Back
Estimated ride time: 30 Minutes to 60 Minutes
Season: March through November.
Good to ride on a windy day?: No.
Start Location: Panorama Point
Drive time to start of ride from Hood River: 10 Minutes
Quality grade of road surface: 10
Overall ride quality: 7
Difficulty: 2

Elevation Profile

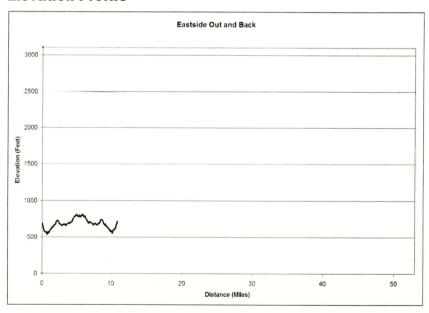

Aerial View

Map

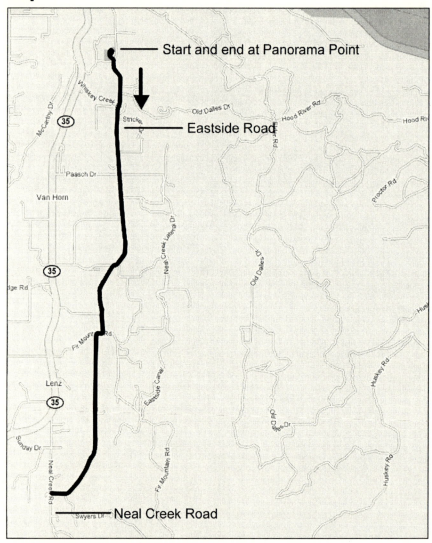

Turn by turn instructions

0.0 Miles: Depart from Panorama Point
0.0 Miles: Ride south on Eastside Road
5.5 Miles: Turn around and ride back to Panorama Point

Glenwood Loop

Description

You'll start at the town of BZ Corners in Washington. This is a 42 mile loop through some beautiful country. You'll ride through forests of Ponderosa Pine, Douglas Fir, Scrub Oak and beautiful meadows and meandering streams, past Conboy Lake Wildlife Refuge and get amazing views of snowcapped Mt. Adams (elevation 12,276'). I've seen Elk in the Conboy Lake Refuge on past rides. Only during the first 4 miles of riding will you see many cars, after that there are virtually no cars on this ride.

Riding the Glenwood Loop with Mt Adams in the background

Ride Stats:
>**Distance:** 42.78 Miles
>**Elevation Information**
>>**Total Elevation Gained:** 2643 Ft.
>>**Starting Elevation:** 696 Ft
>>**Maximum Elevation:** 2367 Ft.
>
>**Ride Format:** Loop
>**Estimated ride time:** 3 to 5 Hours
>**Season:** April through October
>**Quality grade of road surface:** 10
>**Good to ride on a windy day?:** Yes
>**Start Location:** BZ Corners, WA
>**Drive time to start of ride from Hood River:** 25 Minutes
>**Overall ride quality:** 10
>**Ride Difficulty:** 7

Getting to the 'start of the ride'

You'll drive from Hood River to the town of BZ Corners in WA to start this ride. The drive time is about 25 minutes. Cross the Hood River Bridge, head west on Hwy 14, take a right on Hwy 141, take 141 north to the town of BZ corners.

Elevation Profile

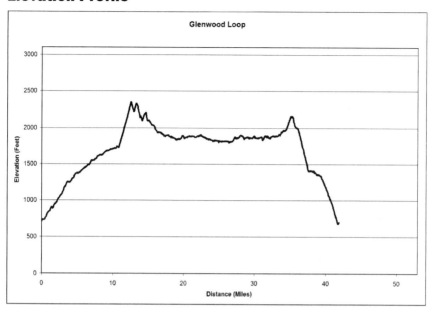

Aerial View

Map

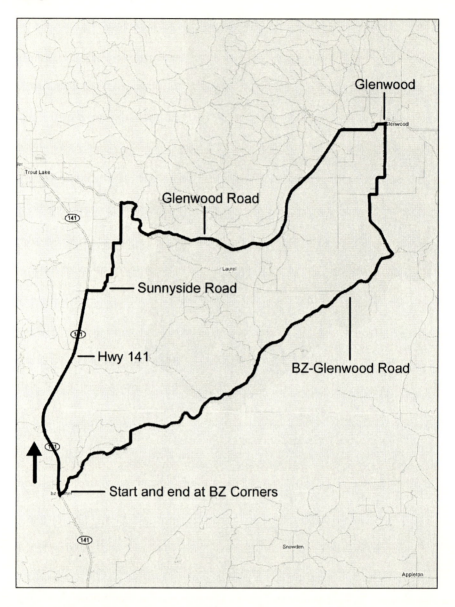

Turn by turn instructions

- **0.0 Miles:** Head north on Hwy 141
- **6.8 Miles:** Turn right onto Sunnyside Road
- **7.6 Miles:** Stay on Sunnyside Road (stay left)
- **9.1 Miles:** Turn right on Warner Road
- **9.4 Miles:** Turn left onto Sunnyside Road
- **10.7 Miles:** Turn right onto Glenwood Road (Trout Lake Highway.)
- **10.7 Miles:** Stay on Glenwood Road until you get to the Glenwood store (Mile 22.6)
- **22.6 Miles:** Arrive at Glenwood Store
- **22.6 Miles:** Go right onto the BZ-Glenwood highway (directly across from the Glenwood store.)
- **22.6 Miles** Take BZ-Glenwood highway all the way back to BZ Corner.
- **42.2 Miles:** Arrive back at BZ Corners

Ride Variations

Combine this loop with the Trout Lake Loop to form a 95 mile 'figure 8' ride with over 6,000 ft of elevation gain.
- Start at BZ Corners
- Ride north on 141 to Trout Lake
- Do the Trout Lake Loop
- Ride South on 141
- Finish the Glenwood Loop

Vista Ridge Loop

Description

This is the steepest ride in the Gorge (let that sink in for a minute.) Steep. Silly steep. Vista Ridge is a gigantic, honking climb that seemingly never ends. Steep. Long. Ok -- you should get the idea that this ride is about climbing. It's also one of the most incredibly scenic rides in the Gorge on some of the most amazing forest service roads in the Gorge. Your efforts will be rewarded with stunning views of Mt. Hood, Mt Adams, Hood River valley and ancient lava flows. You'll also enjoy some of the most remote roads in the Gorge and see virtually no cars. These roads are so remote there is moss growing in the middle of some of the roads turning the roads into a paved 'double track'. Ferns line some of the roads. On the ride down into Parkdale you are rewarded with some very fast, very twisty roads. The road surface is excellent. There is no place to get water along the way unless you want to filter water - so be sure to bring lots of water. The average ascent grade is 5%, but the maximum grade is 19%. There are one or two stretches of 20 yards of gravel roads.

Important Notice

As of 12/23/2007 Red Hill Road has been breached by a stream. Assuming this road outage has not been repaired, you will need to forge this stream with your bike on your shoulder. This will be a 20 foot wide, knee-deep (or deeper) stream of cold glacial run-off with a rocky, uneven bottom (see picture below). In addition, this road failure is at the very bottom of the downhill – so if you decide to 'turn-around', you will have an approx. 2000 ft. additional climb and you're now doing a 60 mile ride. Alternatively, you could do this ride in reverse (clockwise), so you can decide if the stream is crossable early in the ride, vs. at the end of the ride. I personally have had no problems crossing this creek – but others folks have found this stream crossing too dangerous to cross. In the spring or after a large rain storm, this stream could be dangerously high and not safe to cross. I doubt the county will repair this road failure anytime soon. Contact

Discover Bikes for more information regarding the status of the road repair.

Lost Lake Road

Mandatory Stream Crossing on Vista Ridge Loop during moderate stream volume

Vista Ridge Road

Ride Stats

Distance: 36.68 Miles
Elevation Information
    Total Elevation Gained: 4140 Ft.
    Starting Elevation: 920 Ft
    Maximum Elevation: 3662 Ft.
Ride Format: Loop
Estimated ride time: 3 to 5 Hours
Season: June through August
Quality grade of road surface: 10
Good to ride on a windy day?: Yes
Start Location: Dee Mills, OR
Drive time to start of ride from Hood River: 15 Minutes
Overall ride quality: 10
Ride Difficulty: 9

Getting to the start of the ride

The ride starts at Dee Mills. The Dee Mills are located on the Dee Highway at the intersection with Lost Lake Road. To get to the Dee Mills from Discover Bikes in Hood River:
  Go west on Oak Street
  Turn left on 13th Street (heading south)
  13th Street becomes Tucker Road
  Follow Tucker Road going south
  After you drive over the Hood River, bear right onto the Dee Highway
The Dee Mills are approximately 6 miles south on the Dee Highway (You will see signs for Lost Lake.)

Elevation Profile

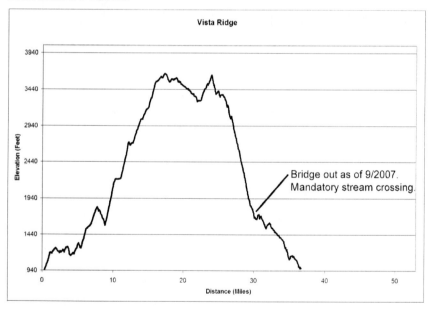

Aerial View

Map

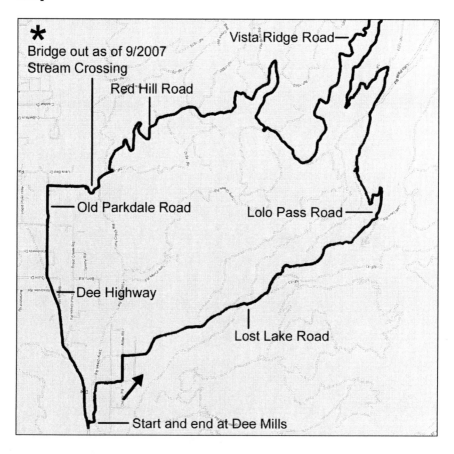

Turn by turn instructions

0.0 Miles: From Dee Mills, follow Lost Lake Road towards Lost Lake

7.8 Miles: Turn left on Lolo Pass Road

~9.5 Miles: Turn left onto Vista Ridge Road (Don't miss this turn!)

At the top of the climb: Bear left towards Red Hill Road (there will be a large paved area at this intersection.)

Follow Red Hill Road down towards Parkdale
Turn left at Old Parkdale Road
Bear left at the Dee Highway
Return to car at Dee Mills

Ride Variations

Start at Tucker Park (this adds 12 miles to the ride.)
Start at Discover Bicycles (this adds 20 miles to the ride.)
If you want even more climbing, do the Lost Lake Loop and connect to the Vista Ridge Loop @ Lolo Pass Road.

Rowena Crest

Description

This is the signature road ride in the Gorge. Assuming you have a day with no wind or light wind, this ride should be high on your list of rides to do.

You'll ride out of town to the east and hit the Historic Columbia River Highway. The Historic Columbia River Highway sits high above the Columbia River and features spectacular views of the Gorge. 6 miles of the ride is on a portion of the Historic Columbia River Highway that is closed to cars. You'll go through the recently restored Mosier Twin Tunnels. You'll pass cherry orchards and pear orchards. The possibility of wildlife viewing is high. I've seen as many as 18 deer on this ride. I occasionally see a pair of coyotes. There are few cars and stunning views of the Columbia River Gorge. This ride also features the absolute smoothest asphalt I have ever ridden on.

The halfway point is Rowena Crest that overlooks the eastern end of the Columbia Gorge. After enjoying the view from Rowena Crest, ride back the same way you came. This ride is an 'out and back'.

For those looking for 'a little more', there is an option to tack another 20 miles onto this ride (see The Dalles Lollipop ride description.)

Historic Columbia Highway

Ride Stats

Distance: 26.98 Miles
Elevation Information
    Total Elevation Gained: 2203 Ft.
    Starting Elevation: 122 Ft
    Maximum Elevation: 745 Ft.
Ride Format: Out and Back
Estimated ride time: 2 to 3 hours
Season: March through October
Quality grade of road surface: 10
Good to ride on a windy day?: No
Start Location: Discover Bikes/Mt. View Bikes, Hood River
Drive time to start of ride from Hood River: 0 Minutes
Overall ride quality: 10
Ride Difficulty: 6

Elevation Profile

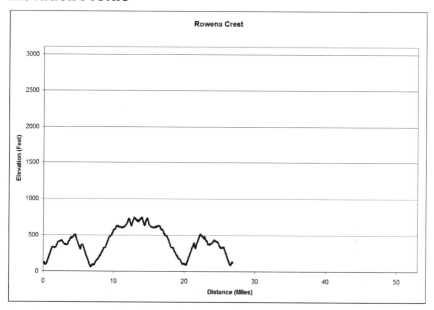

Aerial View

Map

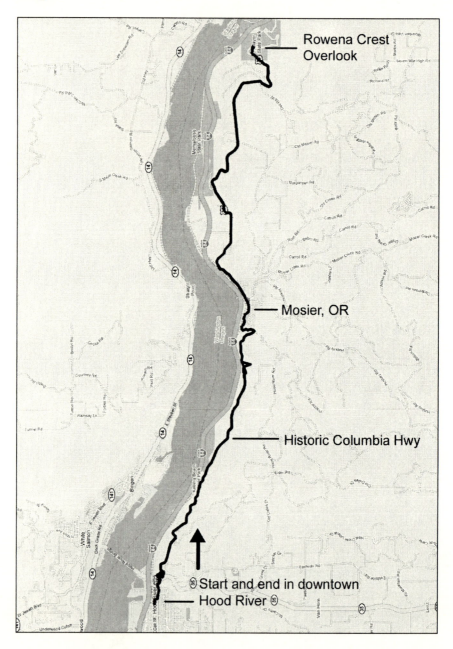

Turn by turn instructions

- **0.0 Miles:** Start at Discover Bikes/Mt View Bikes (116 Oak Street, Hood River, OR 97031.)
- **0..0 Miles:** Go west on Oak Street
- **0.1 Miles:** Turn left on State Street
- **0.5 Miles:** Cross Rt. 35
- **0.5 Miles:** Continue east on Historic Columbia River Highway
- **1.2 Miles:** Stay left on Historic Columbia River Highway
- **6.0 Miles:** Turn left on Rock Creek Road
- **6.7 Miles:** Turn left onto 1st Ave.
- **13.1 Miles:** Turn right into Rowena Crest Overlook
- **13.1 Miles:** Turn around and go back the way you came.

The Dalles Lollipop

Description

At 43 miles and 3000+ ft of climbing this ride has some teeth to it.

This ride starts at Discover Bicycles in downtown Hood River. Travel out of town to the east and hit the Historic Columbia River Highway. The Historic Columbia River Highway sits high above the Columbia River and features spectacular views. 6 miles of the ride is on a portion of the Historic Columbia River Highway that is closed to cars. You'll pass through the recently restored Mosier Twin Tunnels. You'll pass through cherry and pear orchards. One time I saw 18 deer on this ride. I've also seen a pair of coyotes. A herd of about 50 wild turkeys also enjoy this area.

Go right on Marsh cutoff - at the end of Marsh cutoff, go left. Here's the 'teeth' of the ride - you've got a steep 3+ mile climb to the top of this road. Once at the top you are rewarded with a screaming downhill run into The Dalles with virtually no cars. This downhill presents the opportunity to go silly fast. On the way down be sure and enjoy the spectacular view of the valley on the right. At the end of the downhill, go left into the town of The Dalles. There are a variety of stores in The Dalles to get water and a snack. You'll take the Columbia River Highway back to Hood River. You now have 10 miles of rolling terrain back to the base of Rowena Crest. Although the climb up Rowena Crest is steep, it is one of the most scenic stretches of road you'll ever ride - enjoy. At the top of Rowena Crest is a good place to get off the bike for a couple minutes and take in an awesome view of the eastern gorge. From here you ride the rolling Historic Columbia River Highway back to Hood River. There are very few cars and stunning views of the Columbia River Gorge on this ride.

The historic Columbia Highway, east of Mosier

Ride Stats
Distance: 43.32 Miles
Elevation Information
    Total Elevation Gained: 3640 Ft.
    Starting Elevation: 129 Ft
    Maximum Elevation: 1800 Ft.
Ride Format: Lollipop (out and back with a loop at the end.)
Estimated ride time: 3 to 5 hours
Season: March through October
Quality grade of road surface: 10
Good to ride on a windy day?: No
Start Location: Discover Bikes, Hood River, OR
Drive time to start of ride from Hood River: 0 Minutes
Overall ride quality: 9
Ride Difficulty: 9

Elevation Profile

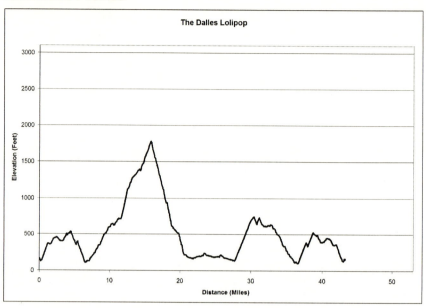

Aerial View

Map

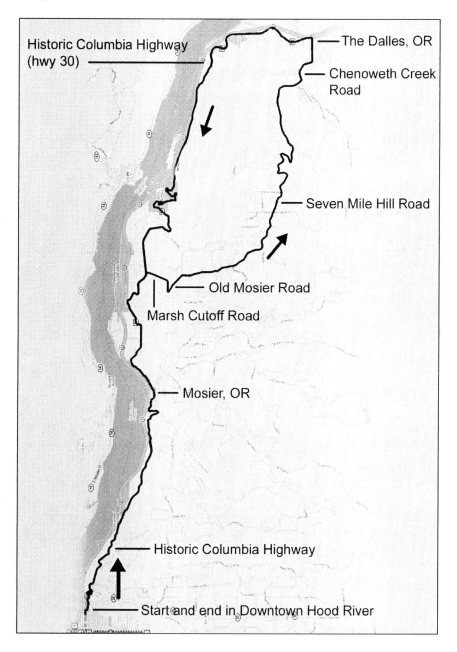

Turn by turn instructions:

- **0.0 Miles:** Start at Discover Bikes/Mt. View Bikes (116 Oak Street, Hood River, OR 97031.)
- **0.0 Miles:** Go west on Oak Street
- **0.1 Miles:** Turn Left on State Street
- **0.5 Miles:** Cross Rt. 35
- **0.5 Miles:** Continue East on Old Columbia Highway
- **1.2 Miles:** Stay left on Old Columbia Highway
- **6.0 Miles:** Turn left on Rock Creek Road
- **10.6 Miles:** Turn Right onto Marsh Cutoff Road
- **11.5 Miles:** Turn Left onto Pioneer Road/State Road/Old Mosier Road
- **13.1 Miles:** Turn right Rowena Crest Overlook
- **14.4 Miles:** Turn left onto 7 Mile Hill Road
- **20.2 Miles:** Turn left onto Chenoweth Creek Road
- **20.9 Miles:** Turn left onto Chenoweth Loop West
- **21.5 Miles:** Turn left onto west 6th Street (Historic Columbia Highway) [you're now back on the 'old highway' – you are going to take this all the way back to Hood River.]
- **32.1 Miles:** Stay Straight (pass Marsh Cutoff on your left)
- **34.7 Miles:** Turn right onto Rock Creek Road
- **34.7 Miles:** Take the old highway back to Hood River.

Lost Lake Loop

Ride Stats
Distance: 33.03 Miles
Elevation Information:
   Total Elevation Gained: 3431 Ft
   Starting Elevation: 950 Ft
   Maximum Elevation: 3324 Ft
Ride Format: Loop
Estimated ride time: 2.5 to 4 Hours
Season: May through August
Quality grade of road surface: 10
Good to ride on a windy day?: Yes.
Start Location: Dee Mills, OR.
Drive time to start of ride from Hood River: 15 Minutes
Overall ride quality: 10
Ride difficulty: 10

Description

You'll be heading up Lost Lake road towards Lost Lake. Lost Lake road is a gorgeous windy road deep in the Mt. Hood National Forest. On a weekday you shouldn't see more than a handful of cars on this 30 mile ride. Although this ride is only 30 miles long, with over 3400 feet of climbing in the first 20 miles, this ride has 'teeth.' On the ride up to Lost Lake, you'll take the 'back way' up Lake Branch road. Lake Branch road typically can not be traveled by cars due to 'mini landslides', large rocks in the road, etc.. The climb on Lake Branch road is some of the most beautiful and remote road riding in the Gorge – absolutely spectacular. You'll then drop down to Lost Lake and loop back to 'Dee Mills. There is a store at Lost Lake where you can purchase food and drink. The first 2/3 of the ride is 'up', the last 1/3 is a fast and windy downhill down Lost Lake road (watch your speed, there are lots of sharp turns and some oncoming traffic.) I've had friends that have seen Mountain Lions and bears on Branch Lake road.

Lost Lake Road

The back-way to Lost Lake (Branch Lake Road)

Lost Lake Road

Getting to the start of the ride:

The ride starts at the Dee Mills. The Dee Mills are located on the Dee Highway at the intersection with Lost Lake Road. To get to the Dee Mills from Discover Bikes in Hood River:

Go west on Oak Street

Turn left on 13th Street (heading south)

13th Street becomes Tucker Road

Follow Tucker Road going south

After you drive over the Hood River, bear right onto the Dee Highway

The Dee Mills are approximately 6 miles south on the Dee Highway (You will see signs for Lost Lake.)

Elevation Profile

Aerial View

Map

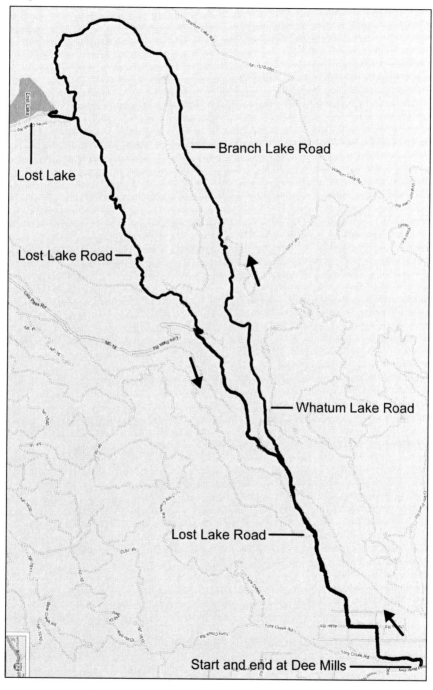

Turn by turn instructions

0.0 Miles: Start at Dee Mills
0.0 Miles: Head southwest on Lost Lake Road (towards Lost Lake)
4.9 Miles: Turn right on Whatum Lake Road
9.2 Miles: Bear left on Lake Branch Road
17.0 Miles: Intersection with Lost Lake Road. (Directions below show how to get back to the car. Alternatively, you could head southwest on Lost Lake road to go to Lost Lake – and then ride back to the car.)
17.0 Miles: Turn left on Lost Lake Road. Take Lost Lake road back to the car.
32.0 Miles: Return to car

Ride Variations:

Do the ride clockwise vs. counter-clockwise.
Start at Tucker Park. This adds 12 miles to the ride.
Start at Discover Bicycles. This adds 20 miles to the ride.
If you're thirsting for even more climbing, ride Lost Lake to Vista Ridge. Connect to Vista Ridge at Lolo Pass Road.

Trout Lake 52 Mile Loop

Description:

The Trout Lake 52 Mile Loop is a spectacular ride on remote roads with fun riding terrain. You'll pedal through the forest surrounding Mt. Adams with many awesome view points. Much of the ride is on a silky smooth 1 lane road with spectacular views of Mt. Adams. Watch out for rocks and large cracks in the road. This is one of the longer rides in the book with 2 beefy climbs. There are no services on this ride (no stores, gas stations, etc.) for 52 miles; bring all the food and water you'll need. This ride is one of my personal favorites in the Gorge.

Riding the Trout Lake loop on a rainy day.

Riding the Trout Lake loop on a rainy day.

Ride Stats

Distance: 52.41 Miles
Elevation Information
    Total Elevation Gained: 4166 Ft
    Starting Elevation: 1953 Ft
    Maximum Elevation: 3941 Ft
Ride Format: Loop
Estimated ride time: 4 to 6 Hours
Season: May through August
Quality grade of road surface: 10
Good to ride on a windy day?: Yes.
Start Location: Mat Adams Ranger Station, Trout Lake, WA
Drive time to start of ride from Hood River: 35 Minutes
Overall ride quality: 10
Ride difficulty: 10

Elevation Profile

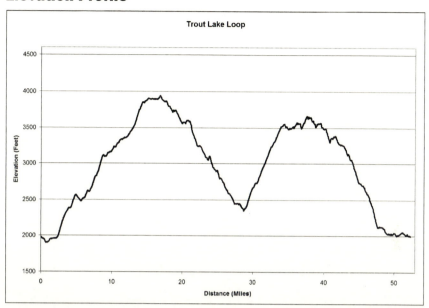

Aerial View

Map

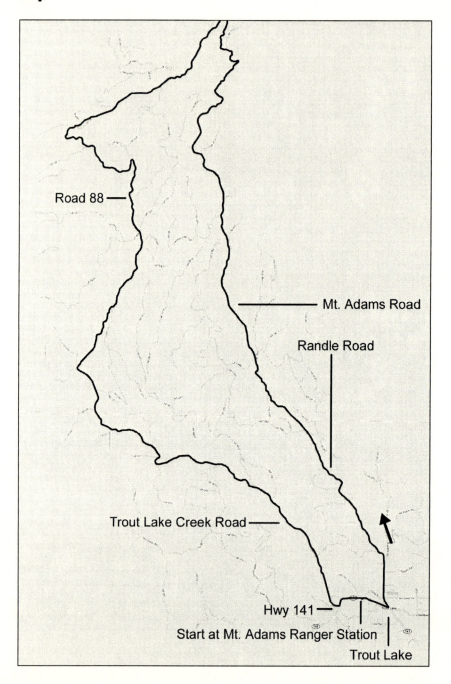

Getting to the start of the ride

This ride starts at the Mt. Adams Ranger Station, 2455 hwy 141, Trout Lake, WA 98650. (509) 395-3400.

To get to the ranger station:

Cross the Hood River bridge

Go west on Highway 14

Take a right on 141. Travel for 22 miles. The ranger station is on the left.

Turn by Turn Instructions

0.0 Miles: Start at Mt. Adams Ranger Station
2455 hwy 141
Trout Lake, WA 98650.
(509) 395-3400

0.0 Miles: Head east on Hwy 141

0.8 Miles: Sharp left onto Mt. Adams Road

2.1 Miles: Bear left on Randle Road (Buck Creed Road). Cross a cattle guard.

28.0 Miles: Turn left onto Road 88 (This is a very important turn – don't miss this turn!)
(Road 88 turns into Trout Lake Creek Road.)

51.0 Miles: Turn left onto Hwy 141

52.0 Miles: Return to Mt. Adams Ranger Station

Ride Variations:

Do the ride clockwise (vs. counter-clockwise.)

Combine this loop with the Glenwood Loop to form an 95 mile 'figure 8' ride with over 6,000 ft of elevation gain.

Start at BZ Corners

Ride north on 141 to the Trout Lake

Do the Trout Lake Loop

Ride South on 141

Finish the Glenwood Loop

St. Petersburg School Loop

Description

This is a gorgeous rolling ride through fields and desert terrain. As you ride past babbling brooks, keep your eyes open for deer, particularly at dawn and dusk. Ride past both working and abandoned barns. Catch glimpses of Mt. Hood. This has very different terrain from most Gorge Rides. This ride has more modest climbing than many rides of similar distance in the book. If you're doing some of the harder rides in the book, this ride makes an excellent recovery ride. We saw only 2 cars on this ride the last time I did it.

Riding the St. Petersburg Loop on a perfect day.

Riding the St. Petersburg Loop.

Ride Stats

Distance: 27.59 Miles
Elevation Information
    Total Elevation Gained: 1403 Ft
    Starting Elevation: 299 Ft
    Maximum Elevation: 1161 Ft
Ride Format: Loop
Estimated ride time: 1.5 to 2.5 Hours
Season: September to May (very hot in the summer)
Quality grade of road surface: 10
Good to ride on a windy day?: Yes.
Start Location: St. Petersburg School, The Dalles
Drive time to start of ride from Hood River: 30 Minutes
Overall ride quality: 10
Ride difficulty: 7

Elevation Profile

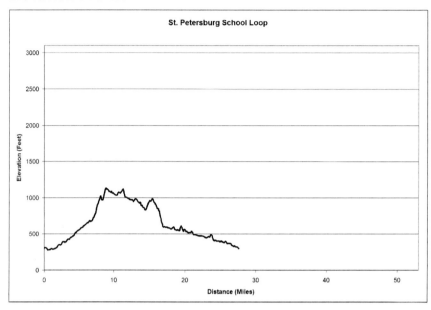

Aerial View

Map

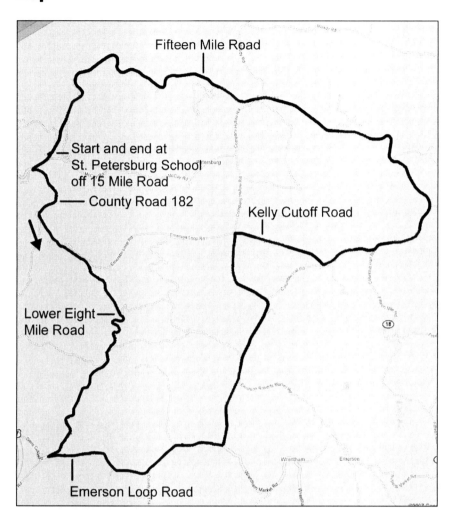

Getting to the start of the ride

The ride will start at St. Petersburg School in the Dalles. To get to the start of the ride:

Take 84 East to The Dalles; about 20 minutes from Hood River

Take Exit 87, US-197 towards Dufur/Bend; stay on 197 for about .6 miles

Go left onto East Columbia View Drive

East Columbia View turns into Fifteen Mile Road

St Petersburg School is on Fifteen Mile Road. It's the first left after McCoy Road.

Turn by turn instructions

0.0 Miles: Start at St. Petersburg School, The Dalles
0.0 Miles: Go west on 15 Mile Road (Lower Eight Mile Road)
0.6 Miles: Go left on Eight Mile Road (County Road 182)
2.3 Miles: Continue on Eight Mile Road (Pass Emerson Loop Rd on the left)
7.2 Miles: Go left on Emerson Loop Rd
10.5 Miles: Go left on Emerson Loop Rd.
14.5 Miles: Go right on Kelly Cutoff
16.1 Miles: Go left on Kelly Cutoff
17.1 Miles: Stay left on Fifteen Mile Road
17.1 Miles: Take Fifteen Mile Road back to St. Petersburg School.

Klickitat River

Description

This ride is a 40 mile out and back: This is the flattest rides in the Gorge. Many of the rides in the book are very hilly. If, after a few days of climbing, you seek a flatter ride, this is a perfect choice. This is an absolutely gorgeous ride running along the mighty Klickitat River. Be aware that the Gorge's predominant west wind does find it's way up the Klickitat all too often making for a headwind on your ride back to Lyle. There are very few cars on this ride.

Klickitat River ride

A majestic Bald Eagle in the Klickitat River valley

Ride Stats

Distance: 40.00 Miles
Elevation Information
  Total Elevation Gained: 1464 Ft
  Starting Elevation: 129 Ft
  Maximum Elevation: 687 Ft
Ride Format: Out and Back
Estimated ride time: 2.5 hours to 4 hours
Season: March through November.
Good to ride on a windy day?: No.
Start Location: Lyle, WA (Intersection of Hwy 14 & Hwy 142)
Drive time to start of ride from Hood River: 30 Minutes
Quality of road surface: 7
Overall ride quality: 8
Ride difficulty: 4

Elevation Profile

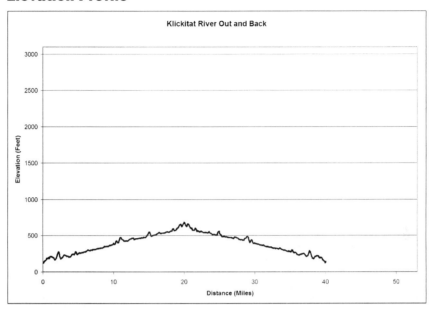

Aerial View

Map

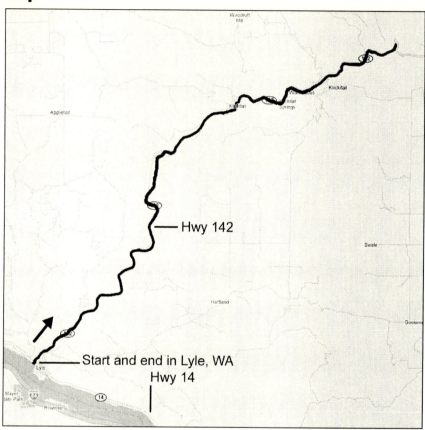

Getting to the start of the ride:

Drive across the Columbia River via the Hood River Bridge
Go east on Hwy 14 to Lyle (11 Miles)
The ride starts at the intersection of Hwy 14 and Hwy 142.

Turn by turn instructions:
    0.0 Miles: Starting in Lyle at the Intersection of Hwy 14 and Hwy 142
    0.0 Miles: Go north on Hwy 142.
    20.0 Miles: Turn around and ride back to the car.
    40.0 Miles: Return to car

Variations

Combine this ride with the Appleton Loop (this will add about 8 miles and 2300 feet of elevation gain to the ride.)

Laurence Lake

Description

This is an excellent 'out and back' ride from Dee Mills to the gorgeous Laurence Lake. You'll ride a modest climb up to Parkdale, rolling through some beautiful orchards in the upper valley. The last 3-4 miles of road up to Laurence Lake is very lightly traveled and remote. As of summer 2007, there has been minor road damage so there are a few 100 yard stretches of gravel road. The expected etiquette is to ride the Dee Highway single-file as a courtesy to car traffic.

Laurence Lake Road

The road down from Laurence Lake

Getting to the start of the ride:

This ride starts at the Dee Mills. The Dee Mills are located on the Dee Highway at the intersection with Lost Lake Road. To get to the Dee Mills from Discover Bikes in Hood River:

Go west on Oak Street

Turn left on 13th Street (heading south)

13th Street becomes Tucker Road

Follow Tucker Road going south

After you drive over the Hood River, bear right onto the Dee Highway

The Dee Mills are approximately 6 miles south on the Dee Highway (You will see signs for Lost Lake.)

Ride Stats

Distance: 25 Miles
Elevation Information
    Total Elevation Gained: 2276 Ft
    Starting Elevation: 958 Ft
    Maximum Elevation: 3016 Ft
Ride Format: Out and Back
Estimated ride time: 2 to 3 Hours
Season: July to Nov
Good to ride on a windy day?: Ok.
Start Location: Dee Mills
Drive time to start of ride from Hood River: 15 Minutes
Quality of road surface: 9
Overall ride quality: 9
Ride difficulty: 8

Elevation Profile

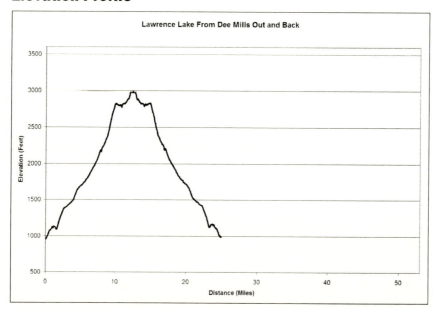

Aerial View

Map

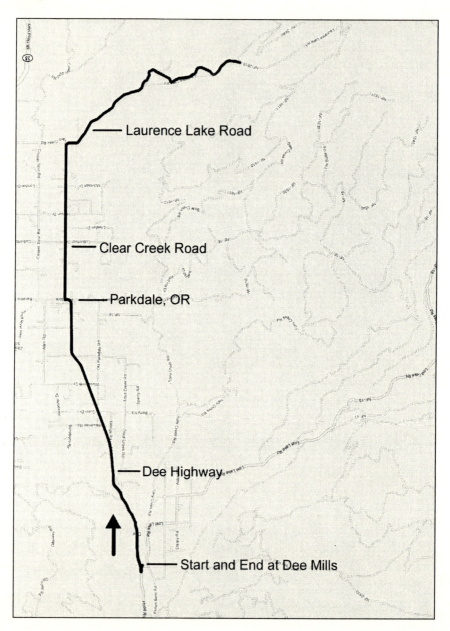

Turn by turn directions

- **0.0 Miles:** From Dee Mills go south on the Dee Highway
- **5.5 Miles:** In Parkdale, go right onto Clear Creek Road
- **8.3 Miles:** Turn right onto Laurence Lake Road
- **8.3 Miles:** Follow the signs to Laurence Lake
- **12.5 Miles:** Turn around and go back the way you came
- **25.0 Miles:** Return to car

Whatum Lake

Description

This is another spectacular ride—one of the juiciest climbs in the Gorge with over 3500 feet of elevation gain in the first 16 miles. This ride features rural forest service roads with very few cars. This is an 'out and back', starting from Dee Miles. You ride from Dee Mills to the Whatum Lake parking lot and then back the way you came. Lots of excellent views of Mt. Hood. This ride is an 'out and back'.

Although I've never seen any bears or mountain lions on this ride, I find myself checking behind me when I do this ride solo on a weekday.

I personally find the Lost Lake and Vista Ride loops are a little more spectacular – but if you've already done both of those, this ride is very similar. Of the three rides, this one does have the best views of Mt. Hood.

Whatum Lake Road

Whatum Lake Road

Ride Stats

Distance: 30.66 Miles
Elevation Information
    Total Elevation Gained: 3579 Ft
    Starting Elevation: 950 Ft.
    Maximum Elevation: 3971 Ft
Ride Format: Out and Back
Estimated ride time: 2.5 Hours to 4.5 Hours
Season: July 1 to Oct 1.
Good to ride on a windy day?: Yes
Start Location: Dee Mills
Drive time to start of ride from Hood River: 15 Minutes
Quality of road surface: 9
Overall ride quality: 10
Ride difficulty: 9

Elevation Profile

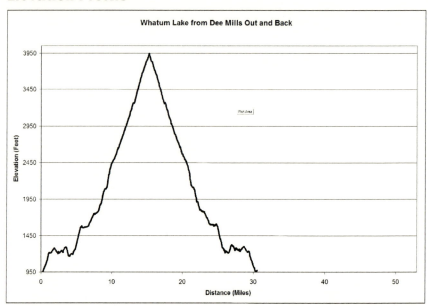

Aerial View

Map

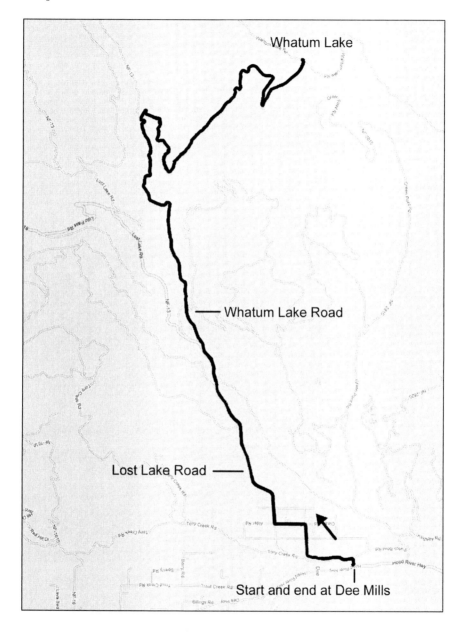

Getting to the start of the ride

This ride starts at the Dee Mills. The Dee Mills are located on the Dee Highway at the intersection with Lost Lake Road. To get to the Dee Mills from Discover Bikes in Hood River:
- Go west on Oak Street
- Turn left on 13th Street (heading south)
- 13th Street becomes Tucker Road
- Follow Tucker Road going south
- After you drive over the Hood River, bear right onto the Dee Highway
- The Dee Mills are approximately 6 miles south on the Dee Highway (You will see signs for Lost Lake.)

Turn by turn directions

0.0 Miles: Start at Dee Mills
0.0 Miles: Head southwest on Lost Lake Road (towards Lost Lake)
4.9 Miles: Turn right on Whatum Lake Road
9.2 Miles: Bear right, following the signs to Whatum Lake
15.33 Miles: Arrive at the Whatum Lake parking lot
15.33 Miles: Turn around and ride back the way you came
30.66 Miles: Return to car

Ride Variations

Start at Tucker Park. This adds 12 miles to the ride.
Start at Discover Bicycles. This adds 20 miles to the ride.
If you want even more climbing, ride to Whatum Lake and then Lost Lake.
For a 'monster' day of climbing (9000+ ft), ride Whatum Lake to Lost Lake to Vista Ridge.

Odell Loop

Description

This is a favorite 'staple ride' of local Hood River riders. You get to ride through the fruit orchards on the east side of the valley and are treated to exceptional views of Hood River Valley and Mt. Hood.

Ride Stats

Distance: 18.7 Miles
Elevation Information
    Total Elevation Gained: 1378 Ft
    Starting Elevation: 142 Ft
    Maximum Elevation: 800 Ft
Ride Format: Loop
Estimated ride time: 1.5 to 2 Hours
Season: March through November.
Good to ride on a windy day?: No.
Start Location: Discover Bikes/Mt. View Bikes, Hood River
Drive time to start of ride from Hood River: 0 Minutes
Quality of road surface: 7
Overall ride quality: 6
Difficulty: 6

Elevation Profile

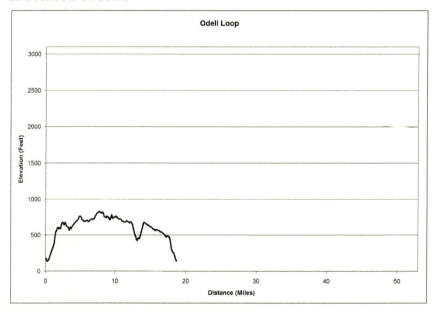

Aerial View

Map

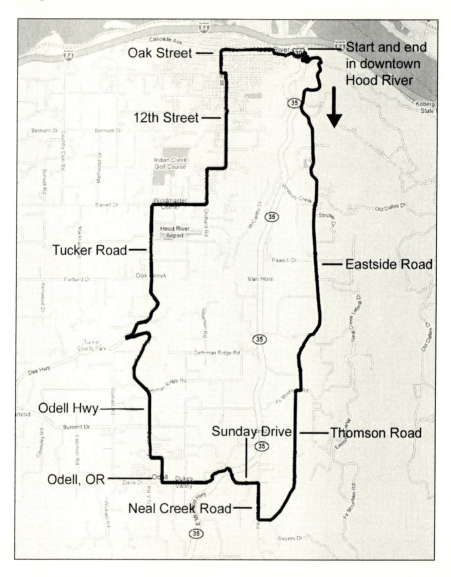

Turn by turn instructions

- **0.0 Miles:** Start at Discover Bikes/Mt. View Bikes (116 Oak Street, Hood River, OR 97031
- **0.0 Miles:** Go west on Oak Street
- **0.1 Miles:** Turn left on State Street
- **0.5 Miles:** Cross Hwy 35
- **0.5 Miles:** Continue east on Historic Columbia River Highway
- **1.2 Miles:** Turn right on Highline Road
- **6.1 Miles:** Turn right on Fir Mt. Road
- **6.2 Miles:** Turn left on Thomsen Road
- **8.2 Miles:** Turn right on Neal Creek Road
- **8.7 Miles:** Turn left on Sunday Drive
- **9.2 Miles:** Turn left on Highway 35
- **9.4 Miles:** Turn right on Davis Drive
- **10.2 Miles:** Turn right on the Odell Highway
- **12.8 Miles:** Turn right on Tucker Road
- **13.8 Miles:** Turn right (still Tucker Road)
- **13.8 Miles:** (Tucker Road will turn into 12th Street)
- **16.5 Miles:** Left on May Street
- **16.6 Miles:** Turn right on 13th Street
- **16.9 Miles:** Turn right on Oak Street
- **17.9 Miles:** Return to Discover Bikes

Goldendale Loop

Description

This is the longest ride in the book and travels through some beautiful country. Enjoy views of Mt Adams, the Klickitat River and the high desert. For the first 20 miles, you will roll along the Klickitat River. At mile 20, you have a healthy 1500+ ft climb on a remote single lane road overlooking a majestic canyon. After the climb, you'll have 20 miles of relatively flat riding into Goldendale and then a fast downhill back to Lyle. Goldendale is a good place to get a snack and some water. Keep your eyes open for bald eagles at the top of the evergreens along the Klickitat River. You should see very few cars on this loop. The Goldendale Loop is a really magnificent ride.

Flat riding along rural Highway 142

The Klickitat River in a very narrow gorge.

Ride Stats

Distance: 68 Miles
Elevation Information
  Total Elevation Gained: 2890 Ft
  Starting Elevation: 100 Ft
  Maximum Elevation: 1951 Ft
Ride Format: Loop
Estimated ride time: 5 to 7 Hours
Season: March through November.
Good to ride on a windy day?: No.
Start Location: Lyle, WA
Drive time to start of ride from Hood River: 30 Minutes
Quality of road surface: 7
Overall ride quality: 9
Difficulty: 8

Elevation Profile

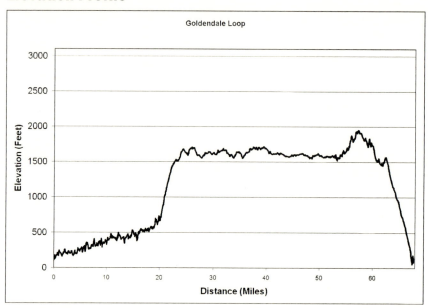

Aerial View

Map

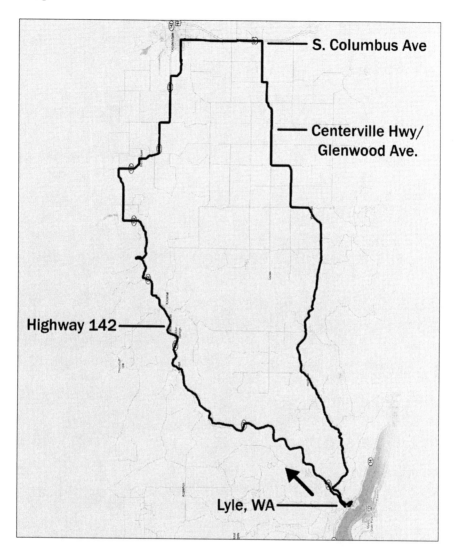

Turn by turn instructions

0.0 Miles: Start in Lyle. Take Hwy 142 North
23.4 Miles: Right on Highway 142
34.1 Miles: Go Right on S. Columbus Ave.
36.6 Miles: Merge (right) on Highway 97 heading South
38.6 Miles: Go right on Centerville Highway
(Take Centerville Highway/Glenwood Ave. back to Lyle, WA. There are some turns along the way so follow the signs.)
68 Miles: Go Right on Hwy 142

Variations

Do the ride in reverse

Combine the Appleton Loop with this ride for an 85 mile day with approximately 5000 feet of climbing.

Appleton Loop

Description

This is a nicely rounded loop. Enjoy spectacular views of Mt. Hood, the Klickitat River Valley, rustic farms and the Columbia River. You start off with a healthy 10 mile climb with about 2300 feet of elevation gain. You'll then drop into the Klickitat River Valley with some absolutely stunning views and finish with 12 miles of flat riding back to Lyle along the majestic Klickitat River. Keep you're eyes open for bald eagle, especially in the October-December time frame. Pay particular attention to the tops of evergreens near the river. This is another ride with very few cars.

Canyon Road climb towards Appleton

View down the Klickitat River Valley

Downhill to the Klickitat River Valley

Ride Stats

Distance: 28.69 Miles
Elevation Information
   Total Elevation Gained: 2785 Ft
   Starting Elevation: 200 Ft
   Maximum Elevation: 2389 Ft
Ride Format: Loop
Estimated ride time: 2.5 to 3.5 Hours
Season: March through November.
Good to ride on a windy day?: No.
Start Location: Lyle, WA
Drive time to start of ride from Hood River: 30 Minutes
Quality of road surface: 5
Overall ride quality: 9
Difficulty: 8

Elevation Profile

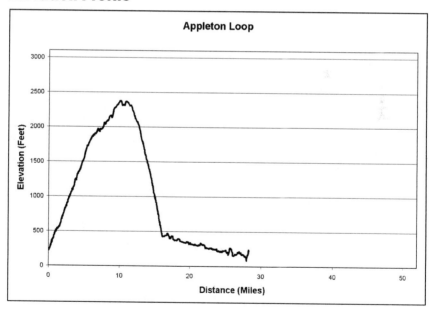

Aerial View

Map

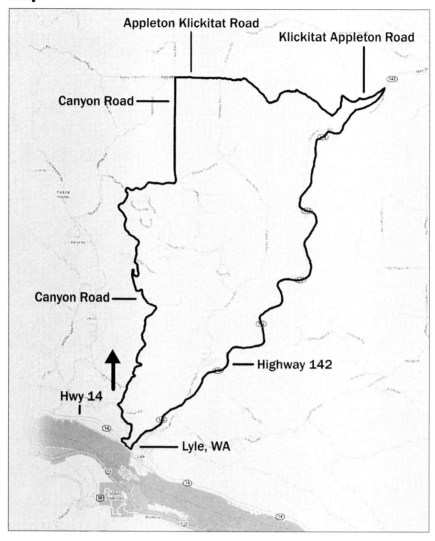

Turn by turn instructions

0.0 Miles: Start at Lyle, WA. Go North on Hwy 142.
0.1 Miles: Go right on Old Highway 8
1.0 Miles: Go right on Canyon Road
11.0 Miles: Go right on Appleton Klickitat Road
17.8 Miles: Go right on Hwy 142
28.0 Miles: Return to Lyle.

Variations

Do the ride in reverse
Combine this with the Klickitat River ride

Parkdale Loop

Description

This is another 'staple ride' for Hood River locals. This ride gives you a meaty 35 mile ride with a healthy-dose of climbing. This ride is a loop along the outer edge of the Hood River Valley. You'll ride through beautiful orchard country with great views of Mt. Hood and Mt. Adams. This ride is similar to the Odell Loop, but bigger. The expected etiquette is to ride the Dee Highway single-file as a courtesy to car traffic.

Ride Stats

Distance: 35.24 Miles
Elevation Information
    Total Elevation Gained: 2200 Ft
    Starting Elevation: 395 Ft
    Maximum Elevation: 1739 Ft
Ride Format: Loop
Estimated ride time: 2.5 to 3.5 Hours
Season: March through November.
Good to ride on a windy day?: No.
Start Location: Discover Bicycles/Mt. View Bikes, Hood River
Drive time to start of ride from Hood River: 0 Minutes
Quality of road surface: 7
Overall ride quality: 5
Difficulty: 7

Elevation Profile

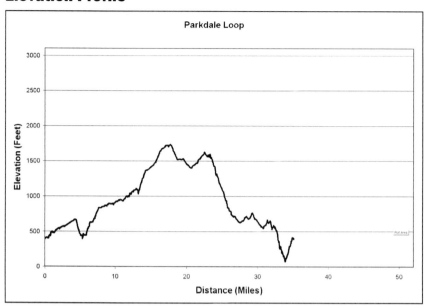

Aerial View

Map

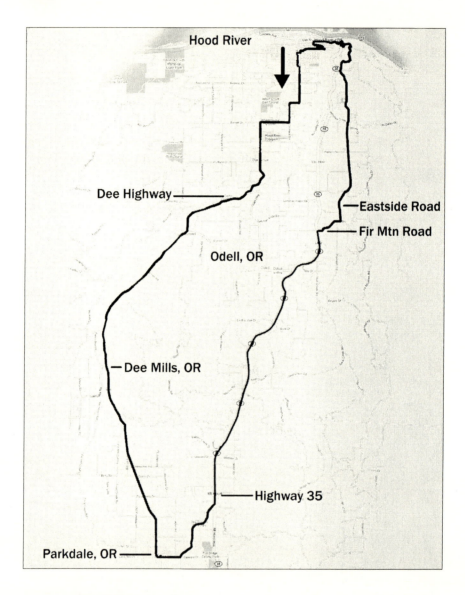

Turn by turn instructions

0.0 Miles:	Start at Discover Bikes/Mt. View Bikes (116 Oak Street, Hood River, OR 97031
0.0 Miles:	Go west on Oak Street
0.7 Miles:	Go left on 13th Street (this will turn into Tucker Road)
3.7 Miles:	Turn left on Tucker Road
5.8 Miles:	Turn right onto the Dee Highway
17.2 Miles:	Go left on Baseline Road
17.3 Miles:	Enter downtown Parkdale, OR
17.9 Miles:	Go left on the Hood River Highway
19.7 Miles:	Go left on Highway 35
27.7 Miles:	Go right on Fir Mountain Road
28.4 Miles:	Go left on Eastside Road
31.5 Miles:	Bear right on Highline Road
33.8 Miles:	Go left on the Historic Columbia Highway
34.8 Miles:	Cross Highway 35
34.8 Miles:	Continue on State Street
35.2 Miles:	Right on Front Street
35.2 Miles:	Return to downtown Hood River

Variations

Add an 'out and back' to Laurence Lake from Parkdale:
    Turn right at Clear Creek Road in downtown Parkdale
    Follow the signs to Laurence Lake
    Adds approximately 14 miles to the ride

Add an 'out and back' to Cooper Spur Ski Resort:
    Turn right at Clear Creek Road in downtown Parkdale
    Turn left on Evans Creek Road
    Turn right on Cooper Spur Road
    Follow the signs to Cooper Spur Ski Resort
    Adds approximately 20 miles to the ride

Add both the Laurence Lake & Cooper Spur Ski Resort 'out and backs' from Parkdale. Adds approximately 28 miles to the loop.

Hood River Lodging

There are a variety of lodging options in Hood River including camping, hotels, and B&Bs. Here are some nice B&Bs in Hood River.

Villa Columbia
Bed and Breakfast
800-708-6217
541-386-6670
info@villacolumbia.com
www.villacolumbia.com

Hood River BnB
918 Oak St
Hood River, OR 97031
541-387-2997, Telephone
541-387-2485, Fax
www.hoodriverbnb.com
jane@hoodriverbnb.com

Inn at the Gorge
Innatthegorge.com
877-852-2385
541-386-4429

If you'd prefer to stay at a hotel, here are a couple options:

Hood River Hotel
www.hoodriverhotel.com
800-386-1900
hrhotel@gorge.net
(right in town, convenient location)

Best Western—Hood River Inn
541-386-2200
(good value)

Comfort Suites
541-308-1000
(new facility, good value)

Columbia Gorge Hotel
(800) 345-1921
www.columbiagorgehotel.com
(very high end)

If you want to camp, check out:

Tucker Park
Hood River Parks and Recreation
(541) 386-4477
(relatively close to downtown Hood River)

Toll Bridge Park
Hood River Parks and Recreation
(541) 352-5522
(a modest drive to downtown Hood River)

Hood River Bike Shops

Discover Bikes
116 Oak Street
Hood River, OR 97031.
(541) 386-4820
discover@discoverbicycles.com
www.discoverbicycles.com

Mountain View Cycles
205 Oak Street
Hood River, OR 97031
(541) 386-2453
mtviewcycles@gmail.com
www.mtviewcycles.com

Hood River Restaurants

Here are some of my favorite places to eat:

Lunch:
Taco Del Mar: excellent burritos
The Taco Stand: authentic Mexican food (across from SubWay)

Dinner:
Abruzzo Italian restaurant: amazing Italian food. Good wine and beer. They serve dinner Tues-Sat.
6th Street Bistro: Great food and atmosphere. Casual bar atmosphere upstairs.
Viento: On the Washington side of the river in Bingen. Excellent food.
North Oak Brasserie: Another excellent Italian restaurant located in down town Hood River.
Brian's Pourhouse: Wonderful Bistro with a hopping nightlife.

About the Author

Clint Bogard (cbogard@gmail.com) has been a resident of Hood River for 10 years. Clint is an avid road biker and typically logs 2500+ miles of riding in the Gorge each year. When he's not riding his bike, he can be found windsurfing on the Columbia River or the Oregon Coast. Prior to catching the road-biking bug, Clint was a committed Mountain Biker, exploring the excellent singletrack riding of the Gorge. This book shares Clint's favorite rides in the Gorge. The following rides are his personal favorite:

1. Trout Lake Loop
2. Vista Ridge
3. Lost Lake
4. Glenwood Loop
5. Rowena Crest
6. Appleton Loop
7. Goldendale Loop

Notes: